Naked In Wonderland

Volume Four

The First 404 Days:
artwork & poetry
in the time of COVID-19

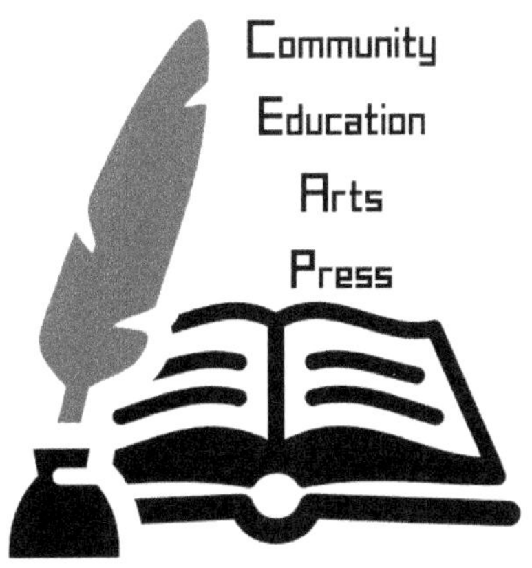

Imprint: *Community • Education • Arts Press*

First Printing: April 2021

Cover design and original artwork: Alys Caviness-Gober
Project design, formatting, and layout: Alys Caviness-Gober
Editor: Alys Caviness-Gober

ISBN: 978-0-9998858-5-7

Published by:
Community • Education • Arts Press
a division of *Community • Education • Arts, Inc.*
Noblesville, IN 46060
https://CEArts.org

Ordering Information:

Special discounts are available on quantity purchases by corporations, associations, educators, and others. Please contact Alys at info@cearts.org for details.

U.S. trade bookstores and wholesalers: please contact Alys at info@cearts.org for details.

for my family

Introduction

In the early days of 2020 came the COVID-19 Global Pandemic, and the entire world changed. By mid-March 2020, due to my pre-existing health issues, I was in isolation at home; here I'll remain, until . . . well, who knows? The entire country needs to achieve at least 80% immunity for people to be safe. That means every American needs to get the vaccine as soon as they are eligible. States vary in eligibility schedules. I'm writing this *Introduction* in April 2021, and my home state of Indiana lowered the age requirement to 55 just a few weeks ago.

As this book goes to print, I've stayed so cautious for one year, one month, and eight days, occasionally seeing my adult children and only grandchild, whilst masked and gloved and socially distant. I haven't been out in public or around other people, because my doctors told me that my lungs won't last a minute if I get COVID-19. Even after I'm fully vaccinated, I'll keep isolated from "the public" until Indiana reaches herd immunity.

COVID-19 is a novel (*ie*, new) corona virus ~ it's a respiratory virus that affects other organs and does not discriminate. Babies, children, old people, previously healthy people ~ all are being affected. The virus acts silently and swiftly. Some people are carriers without ever having symptoms. Some people experience mild symptoms. Some people experience life-threatening symptoms oh-so quickly and go into Acute Respiratory Distress in a matter of hours or minutes. By the time most people are sick enough to be admitted to a hospital, its often too late.

In the past year, social distancing and mask-wearing became the new way of life, at least for the people taking this threat seriously. Far too many people chose to believe the then-President's politicization of this health threat, and they (still) ignore guidelines from the World Health Organization (WHO) and the Centers for Disease Control and Prevention (CDC).

In March of 2020, I started to write this book, the fourth in my *Naked In Wonderland* series. By then, we knew the then-President wasn't going to do anything to protect Americans from COVID-19; his failure of leadership, his lies and purposeful misinformation were surreal in the face of a global health crisis. By May 2020, most of the United States had shutdown, except for essential services. Schools closed. Businesses shut down. Streets were virtually empty. Millions of people lost jobs. Hospitals and medical workers were overwhelmed. There were not enough tests, not enough protective gear for health care workers. The survival of infected people who were hospitalized was low; there weren't enough hospital beds, ventilators, or respirators to meet the number of COVID-19 cases.

Despite reality, Indiana was chock-full of anti-maskers, like many other red states. At the end of July 2020, our Governor finally issued a mask mandate. By August of 2020, the COVID-19 numbers rose exponentially on a daily basis, both worldwide and across the United States: over 4.71 million Americans had positively tested for COVID-19; over 157,000 were dead. Those numbers kept going up in America as the Presidential election loomed, and the incumbent Republican President stuck to politicizing the pandemic. His tax cuts helped the wealthiest get even wealthier while millions of regular Americans and other businesses lost everything.

President Biden won the election in November; on Election Day, he received over 7 million more popular votes than "the former guy". The former guy ramped up his *Stop the Steal* Big Lie that the election had been stolen (despite zero evidence of voter fraud nationwide) and refused to concede. He tweeted and made speeches inciting his supporters to *Stop the Steal*, encouraging the use of violence. On January 6, violent white supremacist insurrectionists ~ followers of the former guy ~ attempted a coup by attacking the Capitol building. Six people died. Hundreds were injured.

In the United States at that time, 28 million+ people had been infected with COVID-19 and over 500,000 were dead.

President Biden was sworn in on January 20, and within a month he accelerated vaccine production and distribution by doing what his predecessor had refused to do: activate the Defense Production Act.

By the end of March 2021, Indiana and many other states were able to open up vaccinations to ages 16 and over; literally a few short weeks ago here in Indiana, we were still waiting for the eligible age to drop below 60.

I garbed up and received my first vaccination shot on St. Patrick's Day, March 17 ~ 366 days since I last hugged another human.

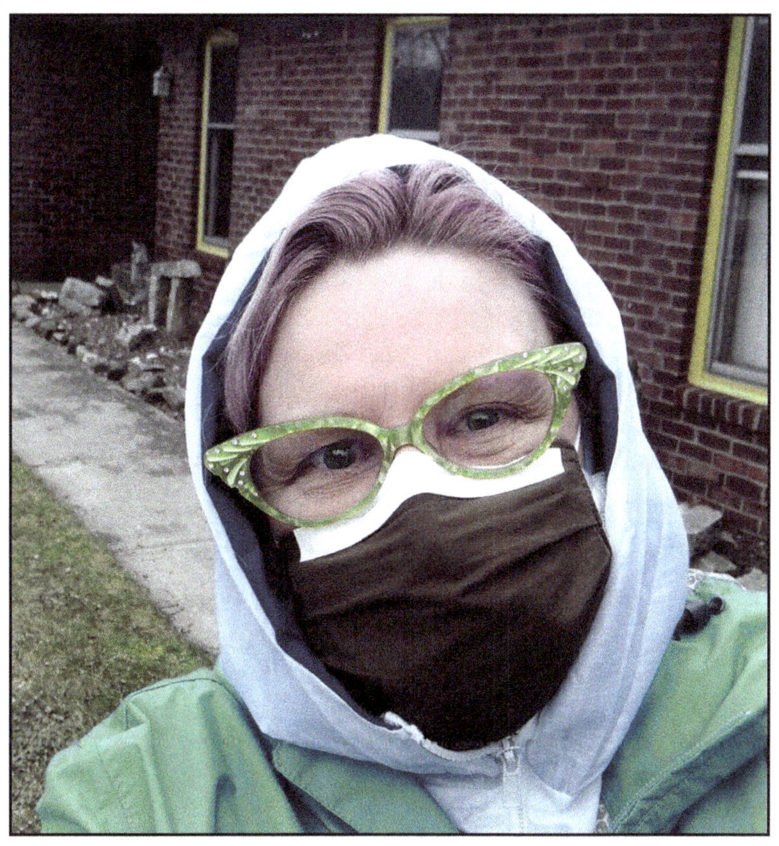

St. Patrick's Day 2021 ~ 1st Vaccination Shot Day

By end of May 2021, there will be enough vaccines to inoculate every single American. Even if we can stop the spread *this* time, COVID-19 has already mutated with several more contagious variants and will come back every year. For generations to come, humans will need booster shots, like MMR, tetanus and flu boosters. For those of us who live through it this time, we're the lucky ones. I feel more confident now about surviving this pandemic, but for most of 2020, I wasn't sure if I'd even make to whenever vaccinations would be available. I owe so much to my husband.

For over a year, he has gone to work masked and gloved all day among co-workers who are rabid anti-maskers. He's grocery shopped whilst masked and gloved, and we've kept away from each other as much as possible in our own home. His protective measures on my behalf have been nothing short of extraordinary.

Part of our "getting through it" plan has been to use Zoom, daily with our son, and our daughter, her husband, and our only grandchild, who turned two years old just a few weeks ago. For the first year of his life, I took care of him Monday through Friday while his parents were at work (on 24 April 2021, two weeks after my final vaccination shot, 405 days will have passed since I've held or hugged him). The 2020 Holiday season was tough. In desperation, I asked my husband if he could turn our foyer, which has no vents common to the rest of the house, into a Visiting Room using acrylic sheets for walls at the openings into the living room and hallway, and he did. It's hard to be "so close yet so far away" but *man oh man* it beats the alternative of not seeing them up close.

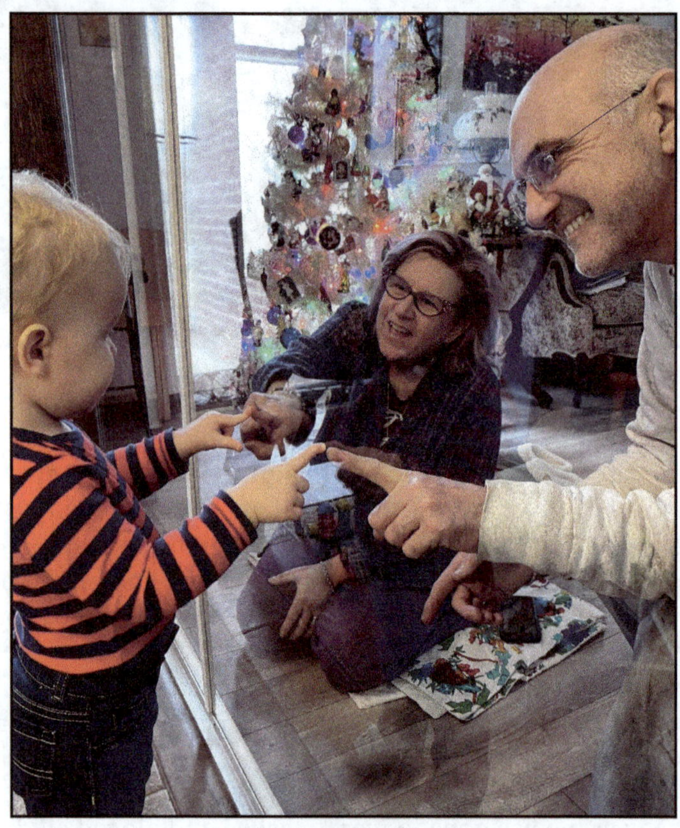

02 January 2021
(photo credit: Evan Dossey, our son-in-law)

We used the conference call function of our home phone handsets (on speaker) to talk to each other as normally as possible through an acrylic wall. I'm so grateful to my husband for building the Visiting Room.

That Visiting Room brought so much joy ~ and even some super-sweet special kisses:

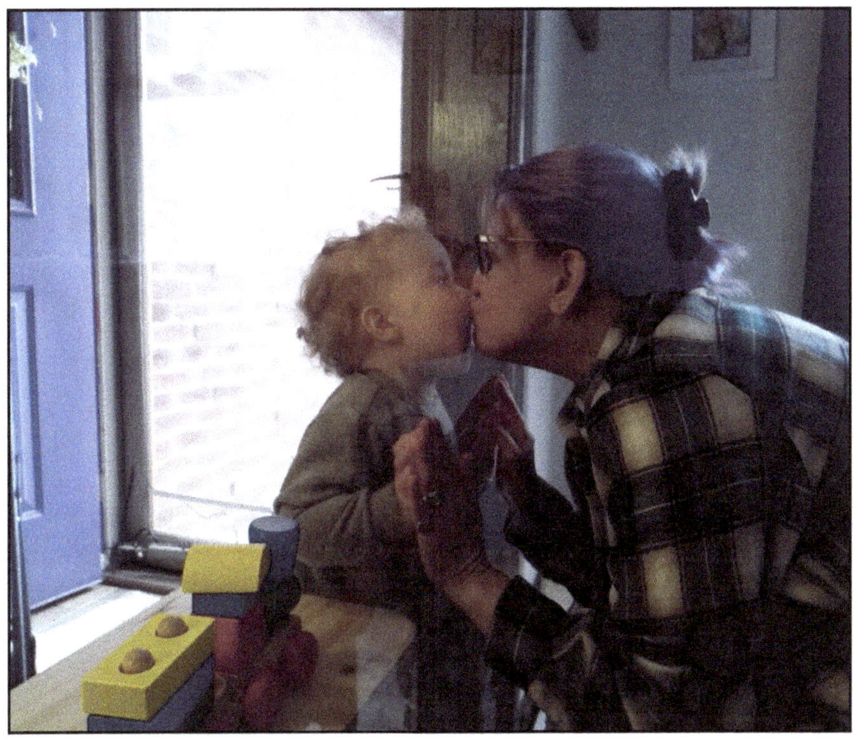

28 March 2021
(photo credit: Cris Gober, my husband)

By late March and April 2021, as the weather warmed, we had more days again where we could spend time outside with our kids and grandson, still all wearing masks and social distancing. Like we'd done last Fall, we had walking visits ~ us in the street, our loved ones on the sidewalks. Our daughter, her husband, our son, and of course the little birthday boy came over and we celebrated his second birthday outside ~ wearing masks and staying socially distant. We hosted our grandson's first Easter Egg hunt a couple weeks later.

On 09 April 2021, I happily garbed up again and received my final COVID-19 vaccination shot.

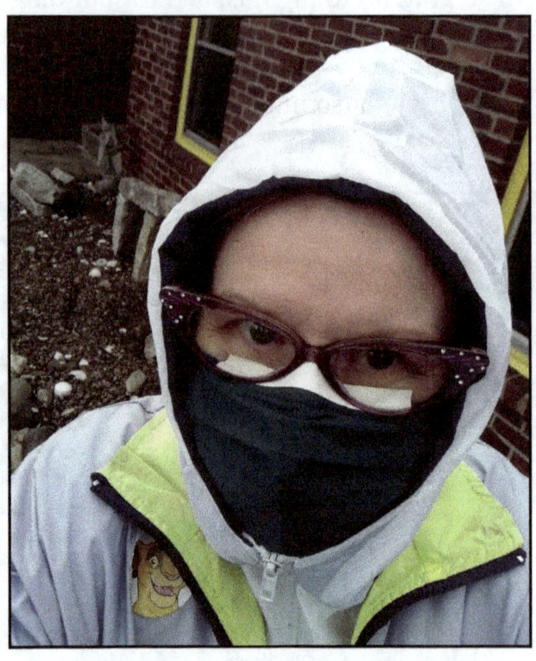

Yep, the past 404 days have been a rollercoaster ride; there were a lot of low moments when I doubted if I'd hug my dearest ones again. The poems in this volume are laid out in the order in which I wrote them: the first few are rather maudlin, written in a sensation of paralyzing fear and sorrow. Others attempt humor and hopefulness; art creations are sprinkled here and there. I didn't paint much last year. Odd, since I had so much time, but inspiration for visual art seemed a rarity.

Hopefully, the poetry towards the end of this book reads happier; I'm happier now than I was when I started this book. My next *Volume* in this series will, hopefully, be full of artwork and poetry created beyond the shadow of a global pandemic. Until then, here's artwork and poetry created between 16 March 2020 and 24 April 2021. One year, one month, and eight days of my life; my first 404 days in the global pandemic. 24 April is the glorious day my immunity kicks in, after being fully vaccinated; I chose that day as the publication date for this *Volume*.

I'm still here.

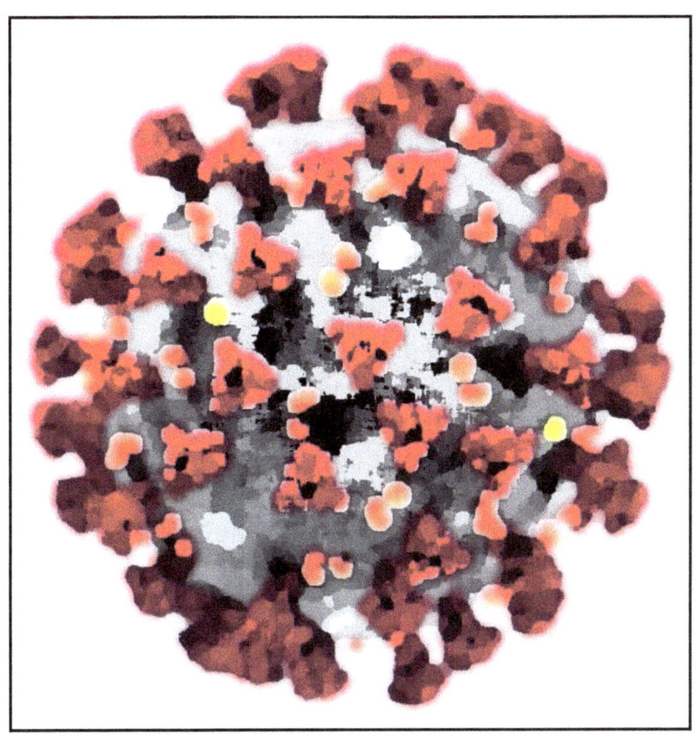

Spring Bloom 2020

Each year,
at a safe distance,
through my windows,
with discontent and yearning,
I watch as the first signs of Spring bloom.

First, a cluster of little white flowers
with small spreckles of oranges and yellows
push up through Winter's gray-brown
debris-ridden soil
and slowly spread;
then a hard green frond
of what will soon be the first tall yellow daffodil,
rising strong
like a standard-bearer waving the brightest flag in battle.
Then comes dozens of tiny bloodred clusters
amidst the first greens of my roses;

they bloom,
the first beauties of Spring.

So brave,
they forge the way
for their late-blooming brethren,
and always seem
incredibly vulnerable to the last of
Winter's icy grasp.

This year's Spring bloom is novel,
like a new story;
it burst forth with
invisible white-gray clusters
sprouted with bloodred blossoms
and even smaller orange and yellow spreckles,
and it spread
wildly
insidiously
moving swiftly
adapting
readapting
deadly
striking down
our most vulnerable brethren,
but soon we know all are at risk.

At first, some of us scoffed,
faith-based believers ironically not believing
in something they couldn't see,
even when numbers came in from China and Italy
and other stricken places,
but then suddenly it was here,
and our numbers grew
a question haunts our minds,
can this really be happening?

We watch from windows
whispering to ourselves
unfamiliar phrases like
social distancing,

sheltering in place,
and handwashing,
and now
reminding each other,
warning each other,
meme-ing each other

we're washing hands obsessively,
we practice six feet of social distance
like practicing dance moves,
following guidance from our dance masters
the WHO and the CDC

~ when have *those* rolled off our tongues??

and we're sheltering
(hiding)
sheltering in place.

This year's Spring bloom is global,
and one by one
entire countries shut down
~ shut down for god's sake
(can this really be happening?)

we're in isolation,
fear-induced paralysis,
we cannot even whisper words like
quarantine
and phrases like
closed for the foreseeable future
because this year's crop
includes a slowly spreading
economic instability
that creeps across us,
hard fronds,
to hold
massive job losses,
rise up
as if held by a weakened
standard-bearer

waving our tattered flag
above a silent battlefield,
as the invasion of our
invisible gray and bloodred Enemy
continues spreading,
always spreading.

These blooms are not
first beauties of Spring.

This year's Spring bloom
is an unsettling gray-brown
debris-ridden time,
a time of free-fall
and chaos,
and for most,
there is no precedence for it
within our lifetimes.

I've always lived in partial isolation,
governed by disabilities and chronic illnesses,

and now

amongst the at-risk most vulnerable,
as this year's Spring blooms,

I watch from my window,

for once content,

behind the glass.

30 March 2020 Setting Up For A Visit From Our Son

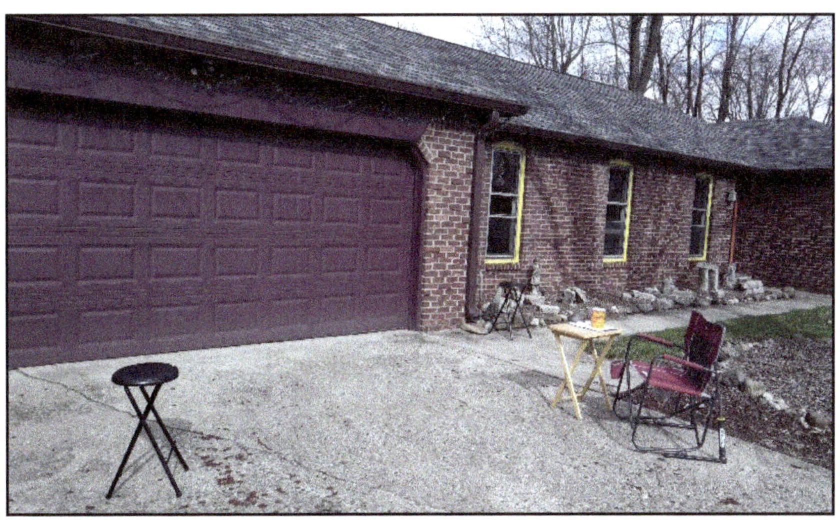

I Don't Want This Poem To Be My Last

Little Paly,
my one and only now,
my Magick Boy,
may I again hold you tightly and kiss your sweet face,
may you be here, again, with Grandpa and me,
may I see your first steps become running ones;
may you come over and fly
around our backyard
laughing and singing your magick songs.
I pray to hold you again,
may you and I once more
have our #backporchlife
cozy together in our rocky chair
as the sweet breezes blow
across our skin;
may we rock the hours away,
watching the swirl of Grandpa's fan.

To darlings who may follow,
may I live to hold you each tightly
and kiss your sweet faces,

but if you only see me in starlight
and feel me in the sun's warming rays,
always
always know:
you are my Precious Ones,
and I see you,
and I hear you,
and I hold you
always in my heart,
always know
you carry my love
forever.

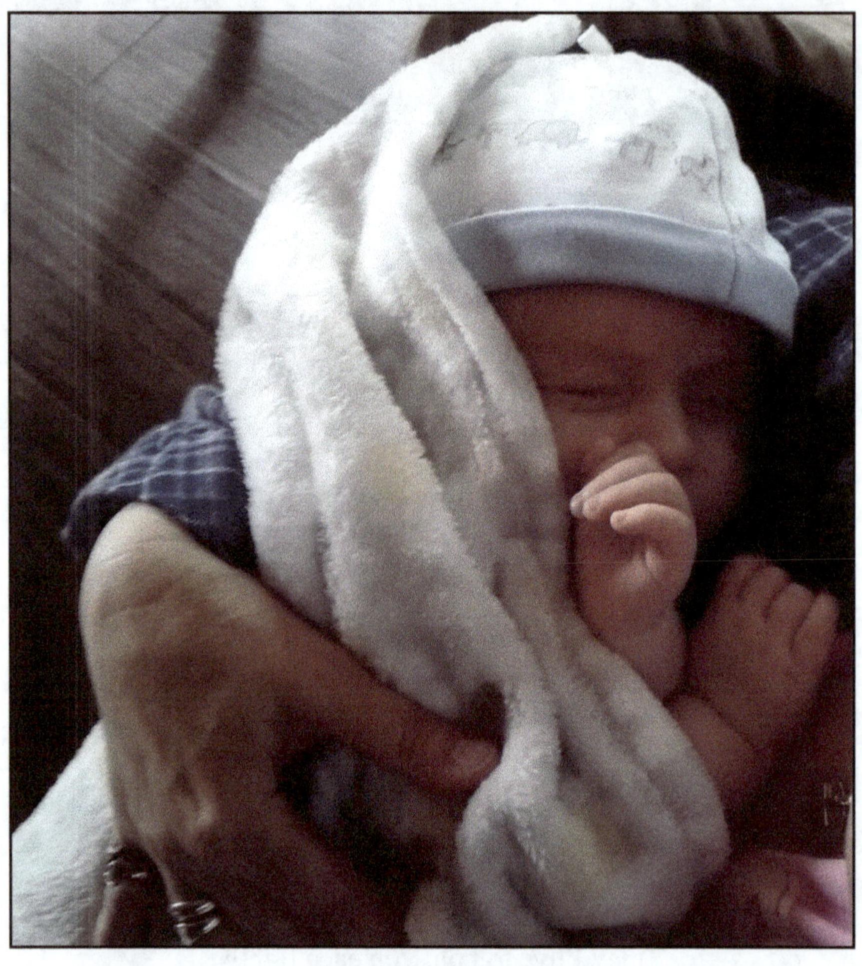

(March 2020)

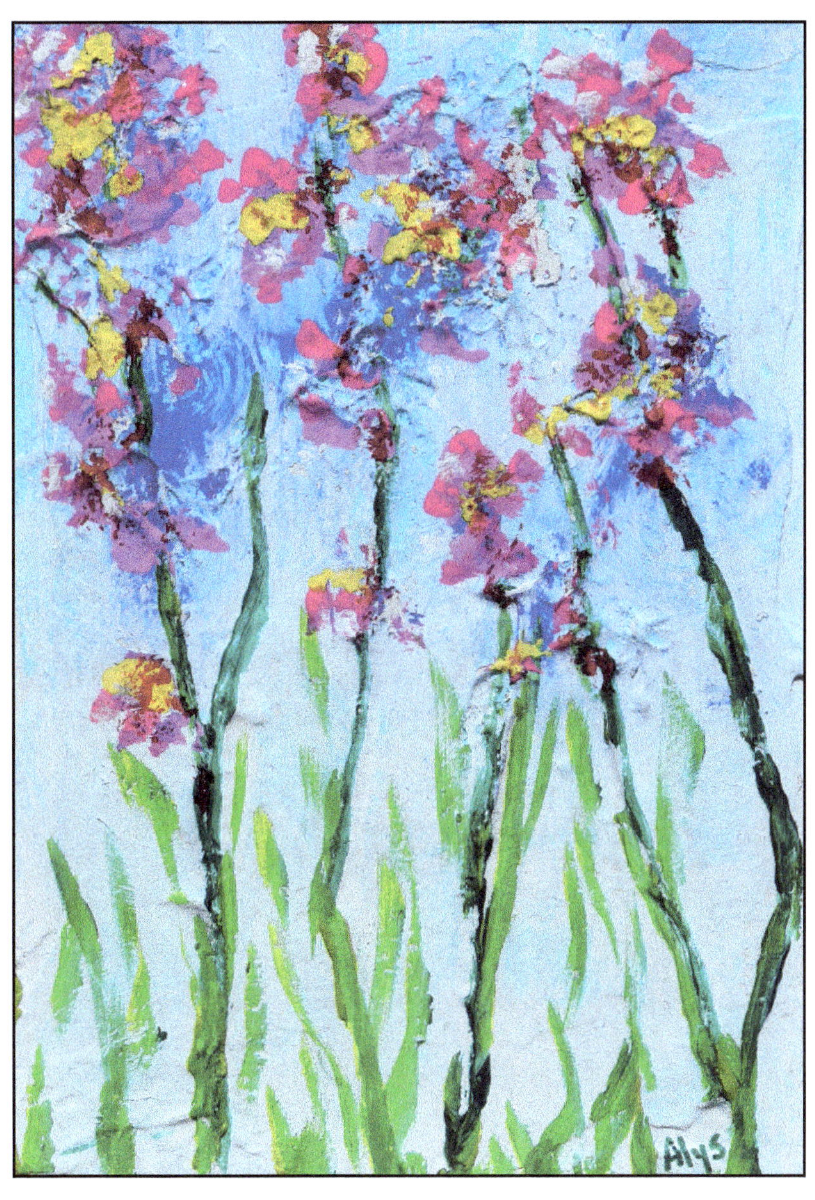

Things I Know

Realizing
my je n'ais ce quoi
has become literal
because
I don’t know what

the future holds
I don't know what
America will become
I don't know what
else we can do
(except try to survive)
then

Realizing
there are things I know

other Springs will bloom
and we'll note
colorful flowers
nodding hello
and we'll sway as
bright green leaves
dance above our heads
and we'll laugh as
tall grasses rise teasingly

and we'll taste
the sparkle of sunlight
in the morning dew

and we'll hear
cotton-clouds whisper
across blue skies
and we'll feel
the day lie upon us
like a warm blanket

and once again

we'll breathe in
stars and moonshine

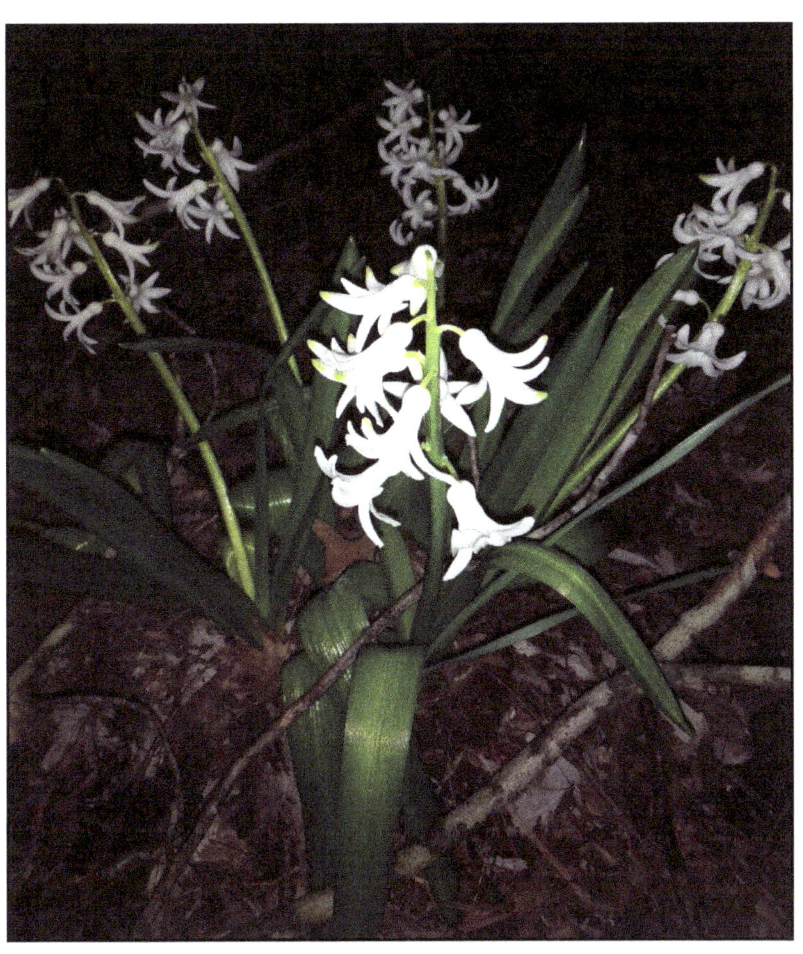

Letter to a Friend

My spirit soared when your words I read
suggesting that we plan ahead
a meeting at a place so favored
where, ere this nightmare tidal-waved
across this land and our lives were flayed,
we'd happily meet and drink well-flavored
insouciant wine or a beer with head
so fluffed and creamy, as we sat and shared
our latest dreams and poems collected.
But O Copper Still's a distant dream!
From pals like you I've had to wean

myself away, whilst in quarantine
I must await the magickal vaccine
before again in public I'll be seen,
the risk's too great, how hard it's been
to stay away, to stay shut in
far from loved ones, who now are seen
only upon my now-treasured screen.

O may doctors soon the vaccine send!
Because each day sees another rend
in the fabric of our communion'd
souls, forced apart, a furthered wend,
as away away we drift forlorn'd,
on oceans of tears from souls so saddened.

May soon our broken hearts mend!
May soon this isolation end!
May soon we meet in person, friend!

Wandering

walking at night
wandering along streets familiar,
yet like everything familiar now
the streets feel like strangers, and
in my quite world along these
darkened empty streets,
walking at night
becomes new

Lines

A song I used to sing haunts my frozen memory
and in the torrents of rainfall beyond my window
run the blurred faces of loved ones far away.

I push aside my cobwebbed fears then remember:
cobwebs glisten like diamonds in sunlight after rain.

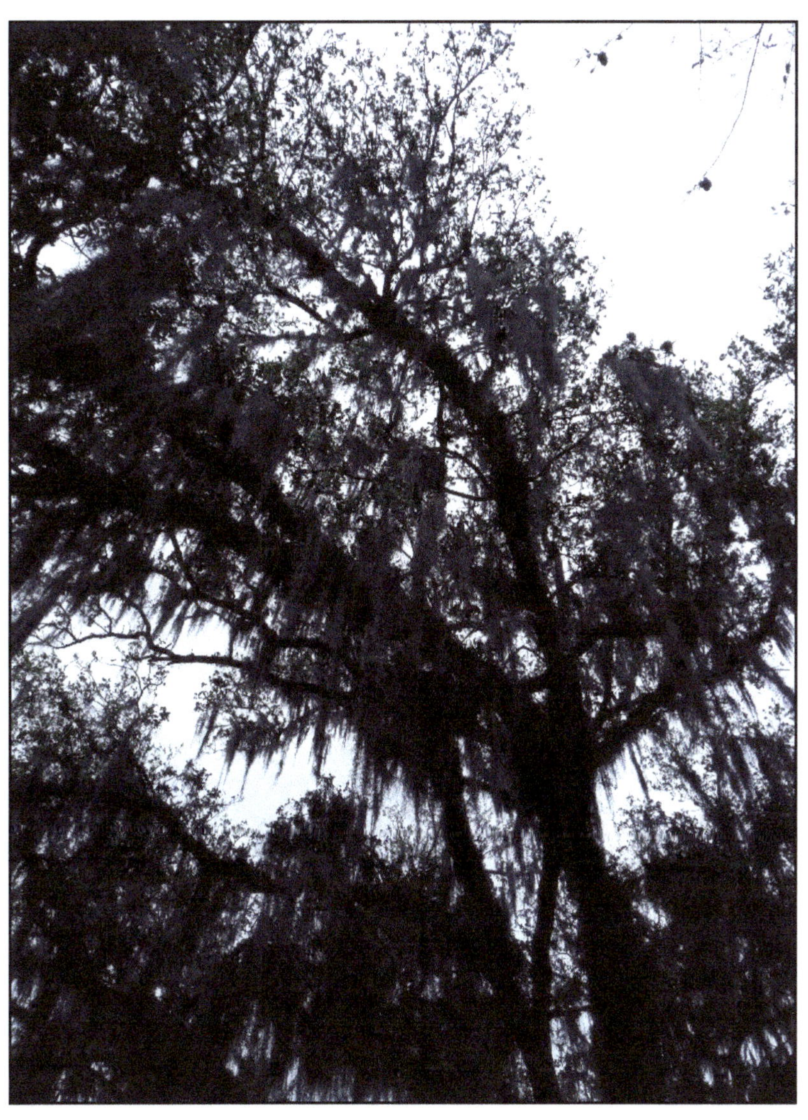

In The Witching Hour

Sleepless, I meander,
down hallways and through
rooms familiar, my fingers run across
beloved treasures left here
bereft of you and
waiting for your return;
I've no need for lights.

Pausing to peer out of windows
into the shadowed nothingness
of darkness accented
in moonlight,
the slim tree branches holding baby leaves
are highlighted softly,
swaying in a midnight dance.

Gathering within me, shadows
and light swirl and cascade in torrents,
I sit before my scrying glass, peering
into the shadowed nothingness of darkness,
my gaze becomes anxious,
desperation filters in;
I seek accents highlighted softly.

Exhale, *let go*.
Stop seeking, *let go*,
Breathe in, *let go*.
Shadows and torrents, *let go*.
Let go let go
and look again.
Exhale.

My breath fogs my scrying glass,
or perhaps for a second
the glass fogs my second sight,
then with swirling cascades of motion
it clears, gently like the swaying
of slim branches holding baby leaves;

I see your face before me.

Sleepless In Quarantine

In a whirlpool of darkness, swirling,
a composition,
mired in this odd exhaustion
born of terror and tedium and turmoil,
birthed by discord and doubt and

the paralyzing grip of cognitive repetition
this is life and death
this is life or death
this is life and death
this is life or death
like floodwaters creeping up and seeping in
or a chalice of desolation overflowing,
becomes an eerie blurring cacophony;
this nocturne's dissonant notes pound out
isolation's senseless lonesomeness, echoing
within this chasm of ever-deepening emptiness,
and sleep eludes.

Black Cat Nights

Some nights, black cat shadows creep
into my subconscious deep,
mewling and clawing monsters
merge in witchey cauldron stirs,
invading my nightmare'd sleep;
some nights, black cat shadows creep.

Glory Days (aka, the Biscuit Queen)

Back in the day (my salad days),
when third shift life
meant days were nights
and nights were days,
I reigned Biscuit Queen
in a fast food joint,
making more and fluffier
biscuits out of each batch
than anyone else ever could;

my Muse, a silvery bowl too big
for my arms to encircle,
embraced ingredients
in scientifically specified order:
first, in pours patented precision-measured

dry mix, forming a mountain,
exhaling like a living thing,
puffing particles up and out
suspending midair then
falling softly;

my brown uniform dims
and my white apron whitens
more, and like a ghost
I work on,
a dusting of unfertilized biscuits
hang on my eyelashes
and kiss my face;

next, I chop a patented precision-measured
margarine brick into butter-yellow cubes
that cling to my fingers,
'til my fingers wave adieu,
waving so they fall away
to disappear into the soft
white mountain waiting
unaware in the bowl;

last, gently slowly pours in
a patented and measured
cold creamy-thick liquid
labeled loudly BUTTERMILK
that pools upon the dry mix
like a cratered lake, with tiny rivulets
cascading down the mountainside;

then with Biscuit Queen magic,
three times quickly my fingers thrust
gently down and then up and around, mixing
just enough to merge the mountain
and cubes and pools into
a sticky wet dough ball,
then fast flop-plop, I fling down
the ball perfectly, centering it
on my wooden board, pre-dusted
with a sprinkle of dry mix,

then rolling delicately,
my roller barely touching dough,
three times my roller rolls,
effervescently cajoling the dough
outward to the demanded depth;

now working quickly
placing and pushing my biscuit cutter,
one smooth motion, down-twist-up-flop
biscuits onto pan, until
no dough is left large enough to cut;

quickly re-form dough ball,
a little drier than it was,
quickly roll my roller
quickly cut down-twist-up-flop
biscuits onto pan, until
no dough is left large enough to cut;

quickly re-form dough ball,
now almost too dry,
quickly roll my roller
quickly cut down-twist-up-flop
biscuits onto pan;
with the magic of threes,
when no one else could get
so many biscuits from a batch,
I reigned as Biscuit Queen.

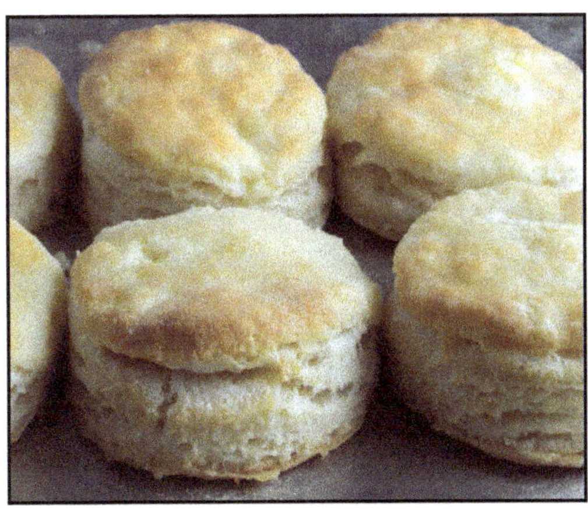

For Mom
Mother's Day 2020

I see you everywhere,
especially in your trees,
I feel you everywhere wafting
on a soft Summer breeze,
like the gentle one that blew
the day you flew away;
then and now,
I feel your loving embrace
across eternity
I close my eyes and feel
your kiss upon my cheek.

Dead Calm

Power's out again tonight;
there's no hum of electrical vibrations
singing their unrelenting
comforting lullaby;
no little (night-) light of mine shines;
TV's flickering glow has faded to a black
as obscure as the moonless views
out my glass darkly windows;
there's no air stirring,
no artificial breezes blow,
brought on not by nature
but by air conditioning and overhead fans.

Slowly my eyes and ears
descend
into the in between;
silence merges with murmurs from just beyond,
and shadows lean upon shadows.

When the power's out at night, I sit alone,
like a ship dead calm on a glassy sea,
waiting, waiting to hear them
waiting to see them.

Summer's Sizzle

Can you hear it?
The gentle sound of leaves
kissing each other,
branches dancing,
as summertime's breeze plays
soft music for them.

Can you hear it?
Floating shouts and laughter,
children playing,
bonding in the splash
of summertime's poolside friendships.

Can you hear it?
The clink of drinks
and music and low murmurs,
gatherings in the dusk on manicured grass,
backyard barbeques expanding
outward into the air.

Can't you hear it?
I can't breathe.

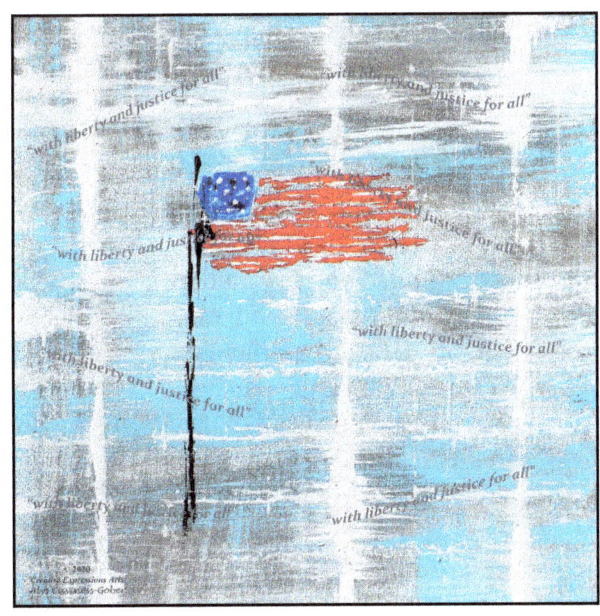

400 Years

What if, instead of 400 years of fearmongering,
What if, instead of fostering otherness,
What if, instead of 400 years of intentional separation,
What if, instead of 400 years of zealous demonizing,
What if, instead of 400 years of sly discriminations,
What if, instead of 400 years of racist epithets,
What if, instead of 400 years of legal inequity,
What if, instead of 400 years of teaching a whitewashed history,

What if America had 400 years of respecting,
What if America had 400 years of fostering familiarity,
What if America had 400 years of intentional unity,
What if America had 400 years of zealous exalting,
What if America had 400 years of dispassionate acceptance,
What if America had 400 years of vocal humanity,
What if America had 400 years of legal equality,
What if America had 400 years of teaching a multicolored history?

What if,
for 400 years,
while America
embraced and cherished,
lauded and applauded,
promoted and supported,
white Americans,

What if,
for 400 years,
America had
embraced and cherished,
lauded and applauded,
promoted and supported,
Black Americans
simply as
Americans?

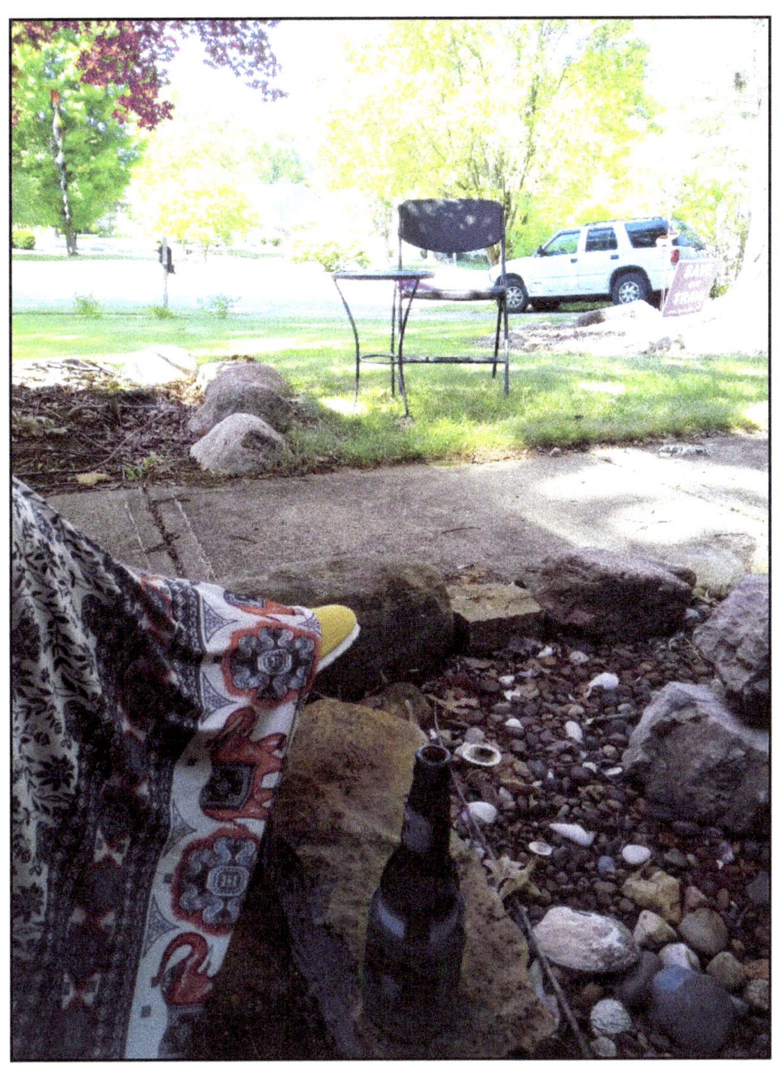

Waiting

I ventured outside my front door
and readied a seat
six feet away from mine,
because my friend was on her way,
which in itself was an amazement,
because since March
I've only seen my friends
onscreen,
and then thinking:

why not sit out here
and drink a beer
whilst I wait?

So there I sat happily,
eager with anticipation
(a friend! in person!)
with gloves on,
wearing my face shield,
and
(of course) upwind
as midsummer's breezy breeze blew
and ruffled the leaves
in the trees overhead.

Eyes closed,
content I sighed
against my clear plastic shield,
grateful that the dancing air
wound and found its way
to the sheltered L-shaped corner
of our front stoop,
and I thought:

someday, someday,
no shields
no gloves
no six feet
and there will again be
lots of hugs

In the meantime,
note to self:
yes, you can sip a beer
under a face shield.

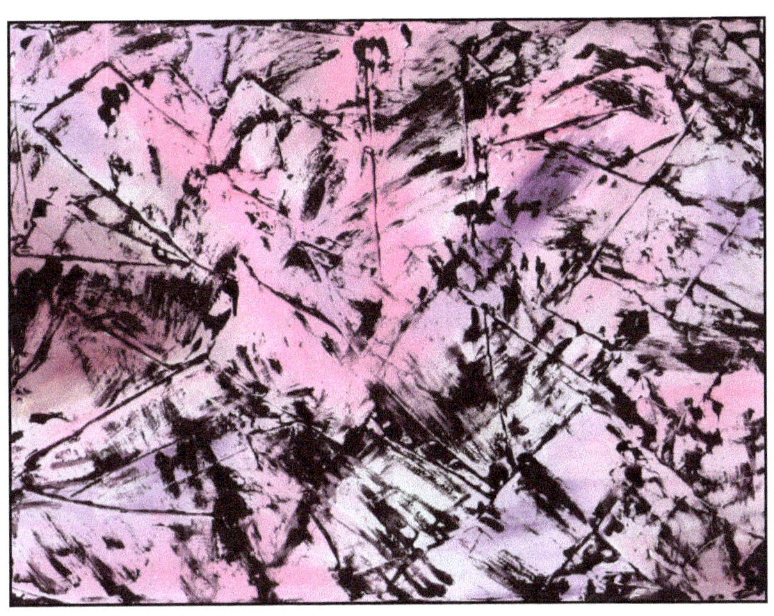

Cracks Appear
(17 July 2020)

This year,
Summer's haze hangs so heavy,
its breath is slow and thick;
the overhead fan stirs down
desolate damp air
into my stifled lungs.
I lounge, hoping for a little sleep
within our screened porch,
eyes closed against tomorrow.

Evening's melody of birdsongs merge
into the mechanical beat
of air conditioners wafting
on humid waves,
and my right foot sways slightly
as if hesitantly keeping time,
to the beat of this different drumming
as it becomes my heart's beat,
then slowly barely breathing
eventually I sleep, just a little.

This day that I didn't want
begins mercilessly;
I drift back slow and thick,
as the rising dawn signals
this day's melody of birdsongs,
this unavoidable day,
and I surrender to it
and cracks appear in
a haze of memories that hang so heavy
like the air
and despite the desolate damp tears
seeping slowly from my still closed eyes,
I can feel my heartbeat
and it is your heartbeat
and I melt
unflinchingly into
this day's embrace.

Rip Up The Floorboards

Shall we
rip up the floorboards?
Thus revealing
where the proverbial bodies
lie buried just beneath
our surfaces . . . .
Perhaps its better
to let them lie there,
resting in proverbial peace,
slumbering just beneath
our surfaces . . . .
Shall we
take in hand our crowbars
and trowels,
and expose what lies
lie just beneath
our surfaces?
Or would that be merely
mutually assured destruction,
a selfish exposé,

excavations of ancient rhymes
and times without
context or compassion?
Shall we
rip up the floorboards?
(I dare you.)

Black Coffee Days

sunrise poking through
swirling nightmares and visions
tastes like black coffee

Epitaph For An Unknown Curmudgeon

Finally, a place with no solicitors allowed!
*(If any durn salespeople try anyway,
don't bother; as in life, I'll not answer.)*

What's The Craziest Thing You've Done In Lockdown?

On social media, a question was posed:
What's the craziest thing you've done in lockdown?

Oh dear, where to begin?
Shall I start with the for-no-good-reason sleepless nights,
or my days-upon-days binge-watching (really bad) old TV shows,
or perhaps my falls-down-rabbit-holes of internet searches
for everything from best cotton bras
(I'm not even wearing bras anymore),
to how to make N95 masks
(which require special fabrics, so down down down
more rabbit-holes),
or maybe my obsession with BBQ chips
(I'm eating them by the bowl-full ***as meals***),
or perhaps I should just regale you with the hours spent
writing lines of bad poetry (not even full poems)
in this never-ending madness of isolation?

Oh, but no, this is a time for honesty,
and so I must confess
mea culpa mea culpa
that the craziest thing I've done,
in full knowledge that I'm not going nowhere
until I can get an **as-yet undiscovered** vaccine
that could be ***years*** away,
knowing that,
knowing *that*
yet still
doing the craziest thing imaginable:

my online purchase,
two sizes too big,
the only size left in Clearance,
of a
glorious
silvery
fairy-queen
ball gown.

Untitled: clerihew

Jeanne de Valois-Saint-Rémy
deserved an Oscar or Emmy
because her role as a *faux* Countess led
to Marie Antoinette losing her head

(Poetry Society of Indiana Annual Poetry Contest 2020,
Premier Poets' Award Category *Reserve* winner)

Ain't It Grand?

Yesterday, thick summer rain fell
hard and fast and straight down,
slicing through July's humid air
like that hot knife through butter,
as thunder rolled overhead
in waves of booming cracks,

like the sky split open, and
then rhythmic aftershocks
rumbled above my roof,
and rain, like machetes descending,
wild and so sharp and sudden,
mushing down my beleaguered roses,
crushed underfoot
as if by some invisible giant
striding past and fast towards some other battle,
slicing sickly branches from my trees,
anticipating destruction and victory,
and I thought,
ain't it grand?
just because
I'm still here.

(Poetry Society of Indiana Annual Poetry Contest 2020,
PSI Grand Prize Category: Honorable Mention winner)

Dreaming Again

Why do dreams feel so real?

Part One

Sometimes waking up is like
gasping to the water's surface
after near-drowning;

straining through blurred vision,
gasping wet-cheeked, dizzily
trying to see a horizon line;

like waves pounding in eardrums
gasping heart and lungs bursting
reverberating sorrow and pain;

eyes and mouth agape with shock
gasping up into grayed silence
clawing at the indifferent air.

Part Two

I lie in silence, pleading with myself
go back to sleep
because both of you were there
back from the dead unaware
of all the days and nights and
the years long gone now;

you were here;
and I wept hugging you tightly one after the other
and you were solid in my arms
I held the bones and flesh of you
like a lifeline
go back to sleep

you were here;
and Mom, you kissed my cheek,
and said, how wonderful to see you
and Dad, you laugh-snorted and scolded
what's the matter with you
my god I heard your voices so real so real
go back to sleep

you were here with me
in the grayed silence of the indifferent air
and all I could do was weep and grasp,
grasping you tightly to me,
feeling the flesh and bone of you in my arms
as my heart and lungs burst
and your voices echoed in my ears pounding
like waves in eardrums reverberating sorrow and pain
my vision dizzily blurred as I awoke, wet-cheeked,
straining to keep you with me
go back to sleep
but my lifelines slipped back
into an horizon I cannot reach
until perhaps a near-drowning
comes again.

Why do dreams feel so real?

80 Degrees In November

It's 80 degrees in November
right here in Indianer
the hottest I can remember
than any year beforer
late Autumn's falling warmer
seems the world's dryer
and we're in a deep fat fryer ~
damn ye, climate change denier!

Wind

marauding winds skitter
overhead across my roof
pirate ships sail past

Solstice Dreams

Comes on Winter dark and cold,
seeping into hollowed nights,
dreams come, unbidden;
a midnight portal opens
and your flowers bloom again.

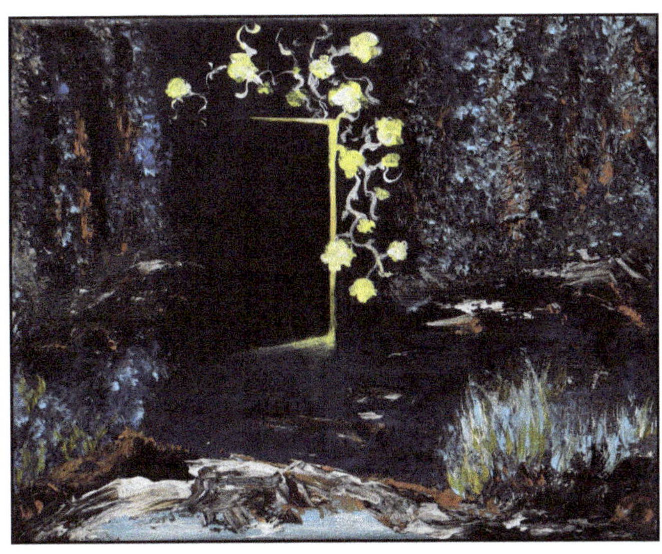

Holidays 2020

Settled cozy, I sit
wrapped in shawls and afghans
made for me years ago
by family and friends,
remembering festive moments and
opening boxes
wrapped in beautiful paper,
remembering laughter and
hugs and sharing happiness;

Remembering, I sit,
settled cozy,
gaze fixed anticipating,
waiting for those chimes,
and that festive moment
when their boxed faces
~ like beautiful gifts ~
abruptly appear and
light up with smiles
and we wave and shout
our *Hiya*s and *Happy Holiday*s
our voices overlapping like
the cacophony of mad thoughts
that crash around in my head
in long dark nights

and we are together
through a distance
incalculable.

Fracture

sleeting ice daggers
slicing open jagged wounds
Time rips like fabric

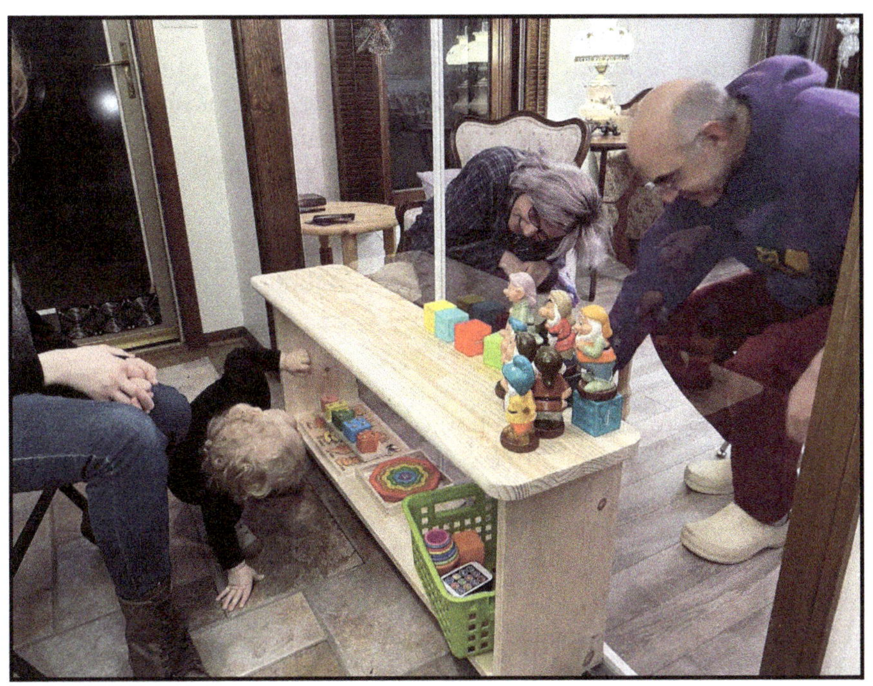

Luke invents a new peek-a-boo game with us.
(25 Dec 2020 photo credit: Evan Dossey, our son-in-law)

'Tis The Season

I

It isn't "out there" mysteriously,
like a mugger hiding around a corner waiting to pounce,
or a drunk driver swerving at just the wrong moment,
nor is it like the flus we've beaten back
with science and annual shots.

It's in *people,*
and a safe bubble is an illusion,
because its potential is in people you know and in those you don't
and in all the people known and unknown to all of them:
when we gather together,
illness and death hang
in the air we breathe in and out.

If only we'd gotten *that* message,
from the start, from those sworn to protect us,
if only they'd included the simple precautions
in their swaggering American brand,
because they knew it's in *people*:
when we gather together,
illness and death hang
in the air we breathe in and out.

II

We're staying home for the Holidays,
they're just more days without our loved ones
joined 'round our tables,

but we'll remember when

~ and wait for again ~

warm scents wafting
of pumpkin pie and roasted turkey
carry thanks aloft in harmless air,

and we'll remember when

~ and wait for again ~

'midst joyous cries and thank yous
as Christmas paper's thrown aside,
and harmless hugs tight hold us,

and we'll remember when

~ and wait for again ~

days of auld lang syne
as many a New Year counts down
to a gentle harmless kiss.

Winter Rain

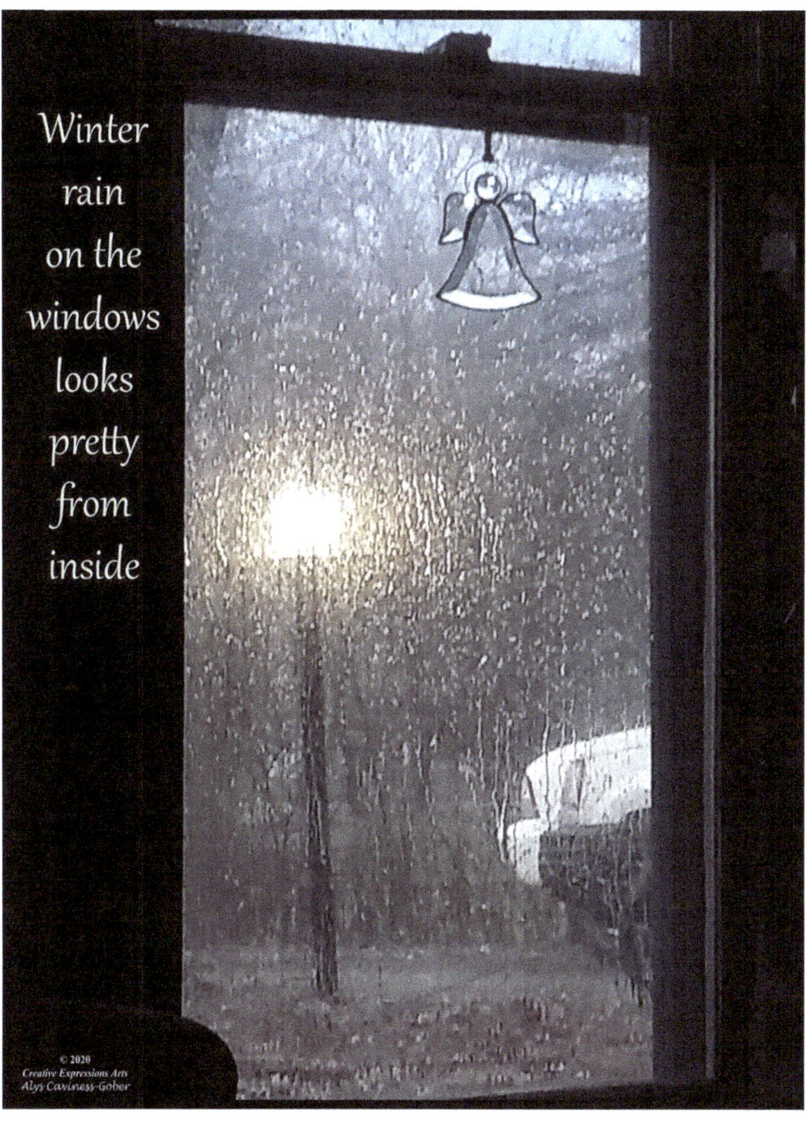
Winter
rain
on the
windows
looks
pretty
from
inside
© 2020
Creative Expressions Arts
Alys Caviness-Gober

Angel Kisses

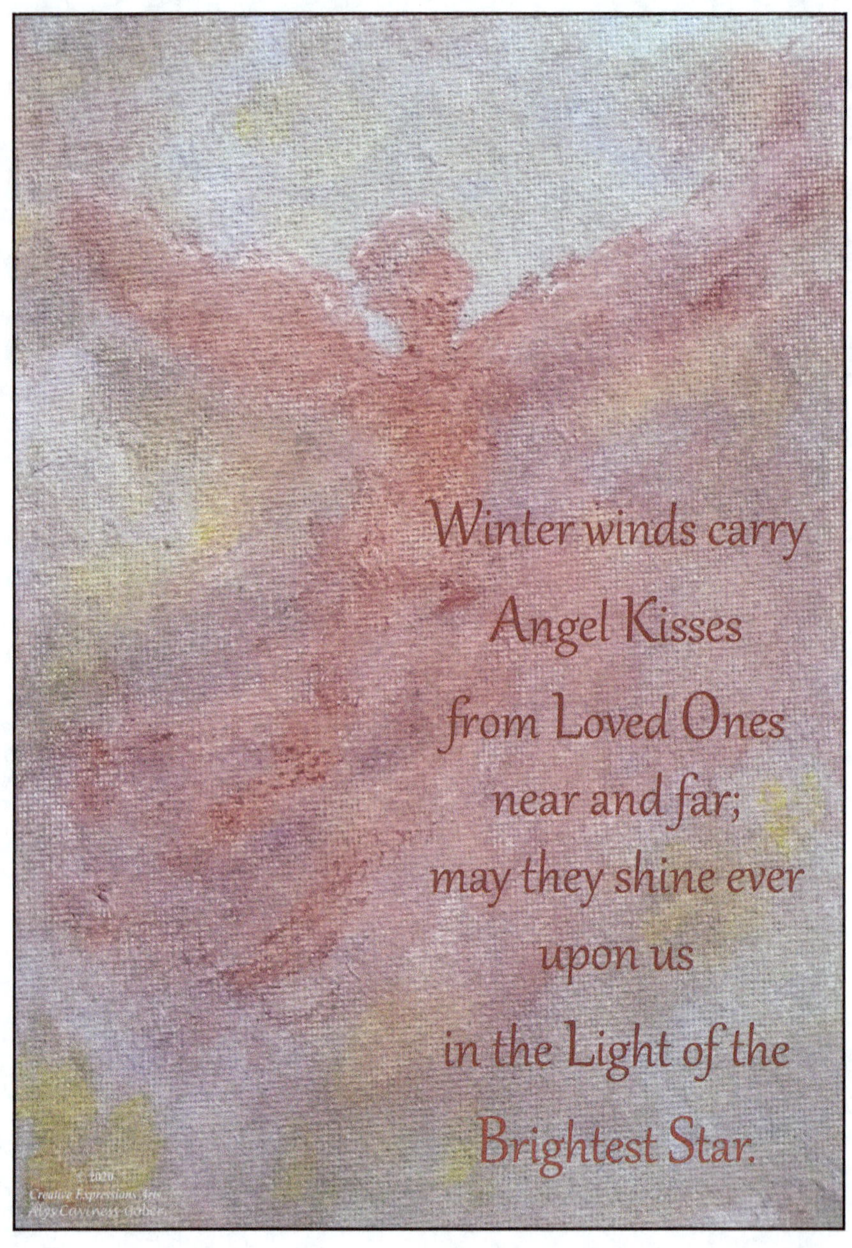

Thoughts For Today

Just yesterday came a steady winter wind,
lifting the tattered flag, hanging listlessly
for so long, with a hopeful flutter,
and an hour or two of cornflower blue sky
meant sunshine had broken through
those heavy-hanging gray clouds.

Apollo, grappling the sun,
stands firm in his chariot,
the flexing muscles of his wild horses
strain, waiting for Aurora to light the way,
and I, awake and ready, watch
through my window anticipating
her stretching and rising
and then she, breathing in and out,
roars across the sky,
bringing forth
this day's fresh colors.

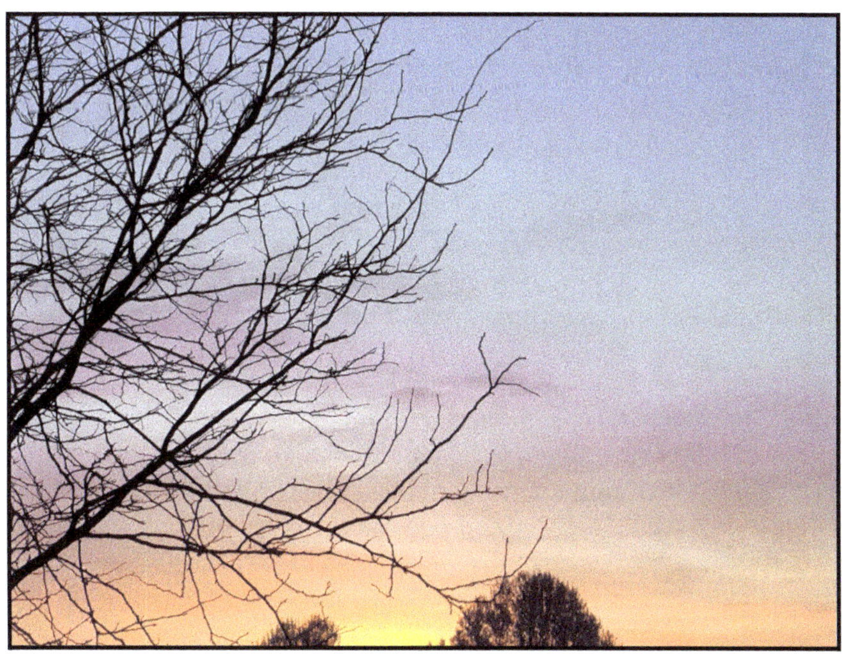

The Soft Snow Fell

The soft snow fell
from a hard gray sky,
floating
steadily
down,
lingering
gently
on
every
surface
like whispered words of love

for Susan & her mother

waves come crashing in
pounding along with my heartbeat
her spirit soars on

For A February Birthday

red cardinal on
a branch outside my window
sunbeam strikes the glass

Even When Shattered

Even when shattered,
with pieces ripping and
bleeding and leaving ghostlike trails
of thin connective disassociated pain;

even when splintered,
with pieces adrift and
scattering, flitting and flying
like the last exhale of a dying butterfly;

even when fragmented,
with pieces exploded
and spreading apart, expansive
like the light of timeless stars in the dark night sky;

even when shattered,
you shine.

Gone (tanka)

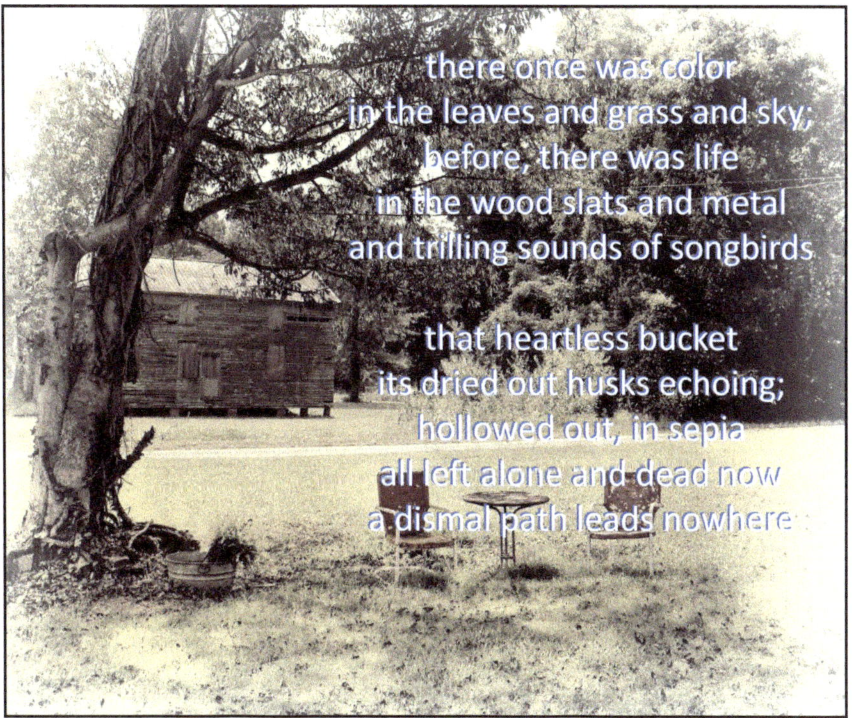

(photo credit: Sandra J. Nantais)

Van Gogh's Starry Night

star lights dance above
swirling night sky deepening
in a corner I weep

A Year of Fairies
(haiku collection)

Rain

steel-gray skies unleash
sparkles of freezing drizzle
fairy wings glisten

Shade

green bowers above
embrace whispering fairies
a shaded rose blooms

Winds

orangey leaves fly
skittering into circles
fairy feet dancing

Snow

pale-blue moonlight shines
upon freshly fallen snow
midnight's fairy sleeps

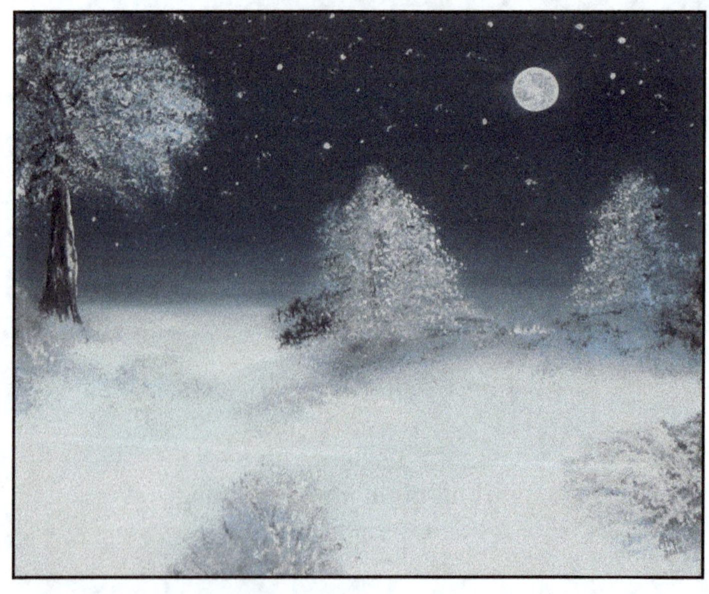

An Ode To My Toes

From October to May
curled
under three blankets,
my toes hide
within two pairs of socks.
From May to September
unfurled
in sunlight's warmth
my toes bask
sandaled and free.

After A March Storm

The soft evening rain
lunies the rising moon
with a pale-golden glow,
and nonny-nonny clouds
drift into midnight dreams.

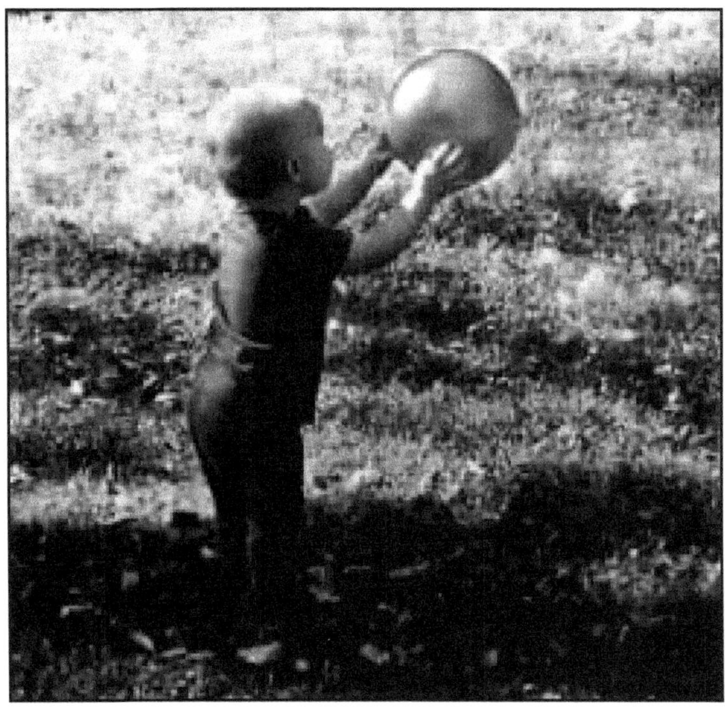

41 Easter Eggs

I hid them, here and there, for
you, nestled in flowers, rocks, and
on the gnarly roots of our old trees,
trees whose Springtime leaves are
barely budding;

soon they'll shade us from
Summer's stagnant air and
perhaps a lazy breeze will pass through
their leafy arms and
brush slightly across our
skin, lifting your curls;

today
I watched you find
all 41 Easter eggs, just like I
knew you would, navigating
through flowers, rocks, and
those gnarly roots with
a sure-footed ease that belies your years,
and we felt the first outstretched yawn
of a lazy Summer breeze.

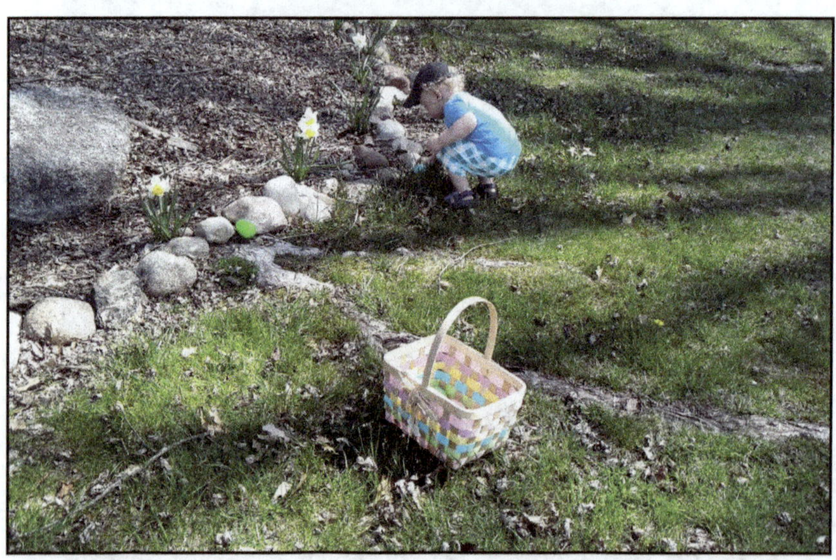

Shifting Sands

wild waves crashing in
onto sun-warmed shifting sands
seagulls crying out
circling low above the earth
wriggling toes remembering

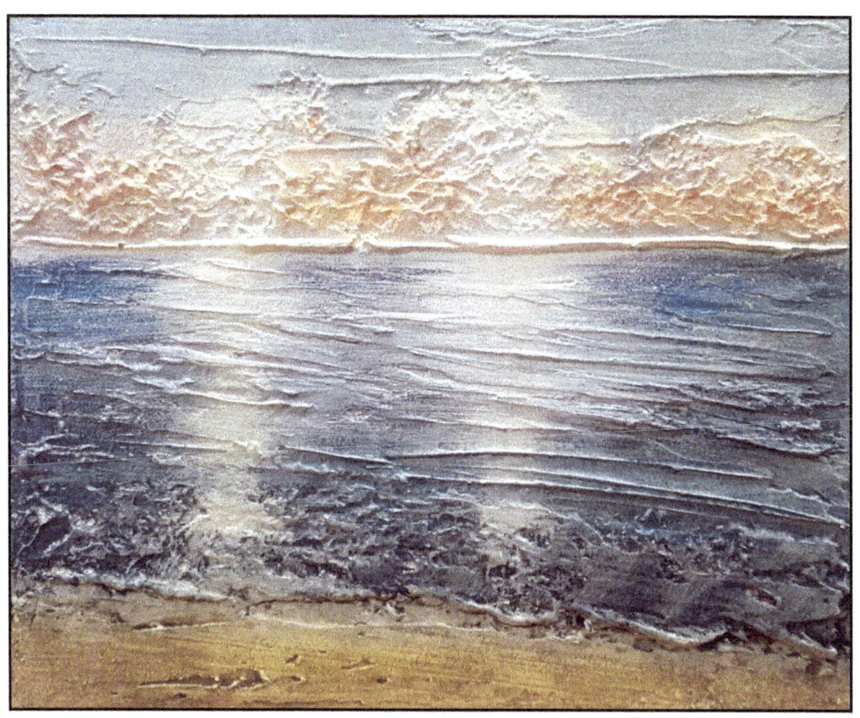

A Gift

Ere the dawn yawns and stretches yellow and rosy over the horizon,
I raise up my favorite cup,
its weight full and its clay solid;
my fingers wrap 'round it in grasping
caress, grasping for its truth and warmth
and security, grasping tightly gazing into today
each day,
ere the dawn yawns and stretches yellow and roses over the horizon.

About the Author

Alys Caviness-Gober is an anthropologist, artist, and writer living in Noblesville, Indiana. Despite lifelong disabilities, she perseveres with art and nonprofit volunteering. Alys' artwork, photographs, and poetry have received national and international recognition.

Alys came late to the life of a professional creative; after receiving her MA in Anthropology, she taught Anthropology and Women's Studies at the collegiate level and was a PhD candidate in Applied Linguistics until her disabilities worsened.

In 2011, she began selling artwork as *Creative Expressions Arts***.** Alys was juried into the *Hamilton County Artists' Association* (HCAA) in both photography (2012) and 2D categories (2013) and served on the HCAA Board for many years.

In 2014, along with author Sarah E. Morin, she co-founded an annual literature-based project, the *Noblesville Interdisciplinary Creativity Expo* (*NICE*). In late 2014, Alys founded *Community • Education • Arts* (CEArts), a 501(c)(3) Arts organization. CEArts offers two annual place-making projects, *NICE* and *The Polk Street Review Project* (TPSR), and diverse digital content, including online *Arts Showcase* exhibit opportunities for creatives of all kinds, and *@theroundtable* arts podcast and short videos series.

Alys is a FY2017 Indiana Arts Commission Individual Artist Project Grant Award recipient, for which she created a series of paintings expressing life with hidden disabilities. She was selected to participate in the *IUPUI Arts and Humanities Institute's Religion Spirituality, and the Arts* 2018/19 seminar class. Alys is a guest film reviewer for *Midwest Film Journal*, and has been an invited presenter at *Poetry Society of Indiana* conferences and Monicat Data's arts and technology *Yellow Summit* (2019). She is a member poet of the *Poetry Society of Indiana* and serves on its Board. In 2020, Alys selected to be a Hoosier poet, with poems included in the State of Indiana's online poetry archive, *INVerse*. Alys serves on the Noblesville Cultural Arts Council and is active in the local arts scene.

www.ingramcontent.com/pod-product-compliance
Lightning Source LLC
LaVergne TN
LVHW020626110826
845149LV00004B/1057

* 9 7 8 0 9 9 9 8 8 5 8 5 7 *